lonely planet
Kids™

BARCELONA
City Trails

Moira Butterfield

Louisburg Library
Bringing People and Information Together

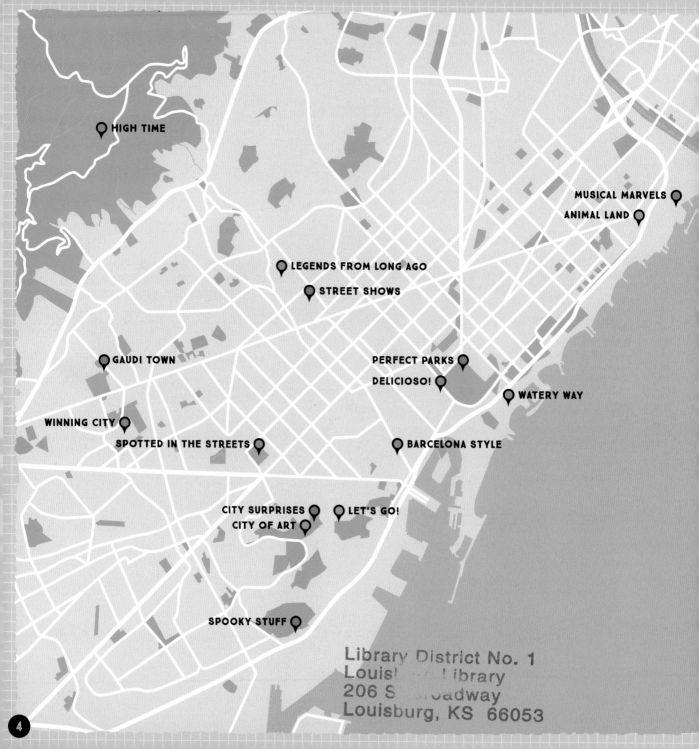

HIGH TIME

MUSICAL MARVELS

ANIMAL LAND

LEGENDS FROM LONG AGO

STREET SHOWS

GAUDI TOWN

PERFECT PARKS

DELICIOSO!

WATERY WAY

WINNING CITY

SPOTTED IN THE STREETS

BARCELONA STYLE

CITY SURPRISES

LET'S GO!

CITY OF ART

SPOOKY STUFF

Hi... we're Marco and Amelia, and we've created 16 awesome themed trails for you to follow.

The pushpins on this map mark the starting points, and each trail is packed with stories from the past, insider secrets, and lots of other cool stuff. So whether you are an art expert, a sports fanatic, or a foodie, this book has got something for you!

CONTENTS

PAGE NUMBER

LEGENDS FROM LONG AGO

Barcelona was first settled over 2,000 years ago, so it's no wonder there are so many legends around town. Take the time trail to find some spots associated with tales from long ago.

START

CARRER GRAN DE GRÀCIA

CASA DE LES PUNXES

SWEET STORY

CARRER GRAN DE GRÀCIA

In 1828, Josep Vidal i Granés, a baker, fell ill in a district of Barcelona called Gràcia. He vowed that if he got better, he would make an annual trip to the St. Medir Hermitage. When he recovered, he set off, and on his return, he threw fava beans to everyone in the street. Why? Because they figure in the legend of St. Medir. Over time, the baker's pilgrimage has turned into a big springtime street parade called the Festival of St. Medir, and instead of fava beans, candy is thrown to everyone on the parade route. There is so much candy, it's called *pluja de caramels* – candy rain!

THE DRAGON DESTROYER

CASA DE LES PUNXES

This medieval-looking building gets its name, which means the "house of spikes," from its pointed rooftop. It was designed over a hundred years ago to look like the kind of castle where a knightly hero such as Sant Jordi (Saint George) would live. Inside, there is an exhibit on Barcelona's favorite saint, said to have been a brave knight who saved a princess by killing a dragon with his holy sword.

RED ROSES GREW WHERE THE DRAGON'S BLOOD WAS SPILLLED, AND GEORGE GAVE ONE TO THE PRINCESS. THAT'S WHY ON SAINT JORDI DAY (APRIL 23), BARCELONA'S ROMANTIC MEN GIVE RED ROSES TO THEIR SWEETHEARTS.

THE TREE TOSSER

PLAÇA DEL PI

This city square takes its name from the pine tree that grows there. Legend has it that a giant once came to the city gates, using an uprooted pine tree as a staff to help him walk. The gatekeepers thought he was going to chop up the tree and sell the wood, so they demanded that he pay a tax. The angry giant lost his temper and threw the tree over the city walls. It landed in the square and began to grow.

PLAÇA DEL PI

KING AND QUEEN OF GIANTS

ALL OVER BARCELONA

Gegants (giants) play a part in most Barcelona festivals, parading through town and dancing for the crowds. They represent characters from the Bible, history, and legend. The city has its own official *gegants*, King Jaume I (James) and his wife, Violant, who always take part in the big La Mercè Festival in September (see page 28). In the 1200s, King Jaume saved Barcelona from French forces and earned his status as a hero of the city. The *gegant* king and queen live in Barcelona's City Hall when they are not parading.

ALL OVER BARCELONA

BARCELONA CATHEDRAL

HAIRY HERO
BARCELONA CATHEDRAL

Wilfred the Hairy is a Barcelona hero who united the region in the 800s and is regarded as the founding father of Catalonia. You can see him carved on the side of the cathedral, fighting a dragon. It is claimed that he killed the dragon and brought it home to show everyone, parading it through the town. He apparently gets his odd nickname because his mother told people he had a hairy back. Thanks, mom!

PUT THAT BACK!
BARCELONA CATHEDRAL

Barcelona Cathedral's full name is the Cathedral of the Holy Cross and Saint Eulàlia, but locals call it La Seu. It is dedicated to Saint Eulàlia, who is buried there. Around AD 303, 13-year-old Eulàlia was killed by the Romans for her Christian beliefs. She was buried in a different church, but centuries later, her coffin was moved to La Seu in a big procession. On the way, a priest secretly stole one of her fingers as a souvenir, but then the coffin grew heavier and heavier, until nobody could carry it. An angel appeared and pointed at the guilty priest. He was made to return the finger, and the coffin grew lighter again.

THE SPOT WHERE EULÀLIA'S ANGEL IS SAID TO HAVE APPEARED IS NOW CALLED PLAÇA DE L'ÀNGEL (ANGEL SQUARE). THE FESTIVAL OF SAINT EULÀLIA IS HELD IN FEBRUARY EACH YEAR.

BARCELONA CATHEDRAL

LEGEND OF THE NAME

BARCELONA MARINA

Legend has it that Barcelona was originally founded by the Ancient Greeks. The story goes that the great hero Heracles and his warriors sailed to the area in nine ships, but there was a terrible storm, and the ninth ship went missing. Eventually, it was found at the foot of Montjuïc, the hill that overlooks the harbor. Heracles fell in love with the area and decided to name it *Barca* (boat) and *nona* (ninth).

MONTJUÏC

BARCELONA MARINA

NUTTY KNIGHT

BARCELONETA BEACH

BARCELONETA BEACH

Barceloneta appears in one of Spain's most famous novels, *Don Quixote*, written by Miguel de Cervantes between 1605 and 1615. In the novel, Don Quixote decides that he is a great knight and travels the country being a fool, followed by his faithful servant, Sancho Panza. Don Quixote fights a joust on Barceloneta Beach against the mysterious Knight of the White Moon. The knight knocks Don Quixote off his horse, then turns out to be an old friend who makes him promise to return home and stop acting so crazily.

ANIMAL LAND

Barcelona is home to some surprising animals. Get ready to spot turtles, snakes, jumping spiders, holy geese, an ancient cat, some Roman pets, and even a Spanish crocodile!

HISTORY OF NATURE

NATURAL SCIENCES MUSEUM

The mysteries of life on Earth are unraveled inside Museu Blau, Barcelona's natural sciences museum. It's home to all sorts of plants and animals, rocks, and fossils.

WALK THROUGH TIME!

The museum's main exhibit is called *Planeta Vida* (Planet Life) and it takes you on a journey from the birth of the universe to the present day. That's a walk of around 13.8 billion years, from the Big Bang through the origins of Earth, the very first tiny microbial life forms, past dinosaurs and the first mammals, to you!

NATURAL SCIENCES MUSEUM

WHEN SPAIN HAD CROCODILES

Back in Cretaceous times, around 100 million years ago, there were crocodiles in Europe. The fossilized remains of a 22 in. (570 mm) long croc were found in a part of Catalonia called Noguera and now live in the museum. Although it's teeny as far as crocodiles go, it's an incredibly rare find.

HOPE IT'S NOT HUNGRY!

The museum's star exhibit is a huge, scary reptile that will eat anything that passes by! Luckily, it lived around 80 million years ago, in the deep sea. It's a replica of the skeleton of a giant marine lizard called a *Prognathodon*. The original fearsome reptile fossil was found in Colorado, US.

SOUNDS GOOD!

DO YOU WANT TO KNOW WHAT ANIMALS AND PLACES SOUND LIKE? THE MUSEUM HAS ONE OF THE LARGEST NATURE NOISE LIBRARIES IN EUROPE, AND ANYONE CAN SEARCH THROUGH ITS THOUSANDS OF SOUND RECORDINGS. ALL KINDS OF NOISES PLAY AROUND THE MUSEUM, TOO. FOR INSTANCE, YOU CAN SHUT YOUR EYES AND LISTEN TO LIFE IN THE MONTSENY MOUNTAINS, NORTH OF BARCELONA, WHILE YOU SIT DOWN FOR A REST ON THE WAY AROUND THE EXHIBITS.

THE MUSEUM BUILDING IS PAINTED A DARK BLUE AND IT'S FITTED WITH MIRRORS THAT REFLECT THE SKY AND THE NEARBY SEA.

KIDS GET A SAY

The museum has a council of local schoolkids to advise it on the best way to stage its exhibits and events.

96,875 SQ. FT. (9,000 SQ M) FLOOR SPACE

4 MILLION APPROX. NUMBER OF SPECIMENS OWNED BY THE MUSEUM

THE LONELY MAMMOTH

CIUTADELLA PARK

There's a full-size statue of a mammoth in Ciutadella Park, and it was once meant to have some friends. It was made to represent a Christian religious belief that extinct animals disappeared from Earth because they hadn't made it onto Noah's Ark. There were meant to be other extinct animal statues but they were never created. Now, the old mammoth stands alone, but children like to keep it company by climbing on its trunk.

CIUTADELLA PARK

THE CLOISTERS OF LA SEU

BARCELONA'S HOLY BIRDS

THE CLOISTERS OF LA SEU

Barcelona's La Seu Cathedral is the only cathedral in the world with a flock of geese! Thirteen of them live in the cloisters, one for each year in the life of Saint Eulàlia, who is buried inside the church (see page 8). Poor Eulàlia suffered 13 grisly Roman tortures, one for each year of her life, before she was finally beheaded. According to legend, a dove flew out of her neck when her head was cut off.

ANIMALS GO, TOO

PLAÇA DE LA VILA DE MADRID

Amid the busy traffic just off La Rambla, there's an Ancient Roman graveyard. Nearly 100 Romans were buried here around 2,000 years ago with their best belongings and their animals, too! Farm animals, dogs, and horses were all buried, probably for the dead to take with them to the afterlife. One grave was more unusual than the others. It had ten dog skeletons, a horse's skull, and six baby pigs in it. Nobody knows why.

THE OLDEST CAT IN TOWN

EGYPTIAN MUSEUM

The Ancient Egyptians believed that humans could live forever in another life and might need their bodies, so they mummified their dead. It wasn't only people who got the full body-bandage treatment. Animals did, too, and one of them – a little mummified cat – lives in this Barcelona museum. It last purred around 2,700 years ago.

PLAÇA DE LA VILA DE MADRID

search: CREEPY-CRAWLIES

📍 SPIDERS

You can find over 1,500 species of spiders in Spain. *Saitis barbipes* jumping spiders live in the Montjuïc Castle walls in Barcelona. These alarming arachnids grow to about 0.2 in. (5 mm) long and have a row of four shiny blue-green eyes. The males have bright-red legs.

BLESSED ARE THE ANIMALS
ESCOLA PIA SANT ANTONI

The Tres Tombs animal festival takes place in January to honor Saint Anthony the Abbot, who is the patron saint of domestic animals. Residents dress up as farmers and peasants and parade through the streets on horses and carts, or leading donkeys. Just before they reach the Escola Pia Sant Antoni (a local school), the animals are blessed by a priest. Residents bring their pets to be blessed, too. Saint Anthony was such a good friend to animals that he once found and healed an injured piglet, which followed him around ever after.

A SLICE OF JUNGLE
COSMOCAIXA BARCELONA

You can go for a walk in a version of the South American Amazon rainforest at the CosmoCaixa science museum. The *Bosc Inundat*, meaning the "flooded forest," is a replica covering over 10,764 sq. ft. (1,000 sq m), and it's home to real Amazonian animals, including alligators, ants, boa constrictors, fish, tropical birds, and even a capybara. To make the animals feel at home, it "rains" every 15 minutes, when water sprays over the forest.

100+ AMAZON ANIMAL AND PLANT SPECIES living in the *Bosc Inundat* exhibit at CosmoCaixa.

THE BOTANICAL GARDENS ON MONTJUÏC ARE A GREAT PLACE TO SPOT FROGS AND HEAR THEM, TOO. THEY LIKE TO CALL TO EACH OTHER ON SUMMER EVENINGS.

TURTLE RESCUE
CRAM FOUNDATION

Marine turtles visit the seas around Barcelona but they can get into difficulty if they get snagged on fishing hooks or accidentally swallow plastic bags floating in the water, mistaking them for jellyfish. Turtles are rescued, nursed, and returned to the wild by the experts who work at the CRAM Foundation, a marine conservation center near Barcelona Airport. The CRAM scientists have rescued local dolphins, too.

NATURE CASTLE
MONTJUÏC CASTLE

The sandstone walls of Montjuïc Castle are home to some unusual Barcelona residents. Little Moorish gecko lizards dart between the nooks, sticky hairs on their feet helping them to climb upside down. Occasionally, Europe's longest snake, the Montpellier snake, is spotted here, too. Montpellier snakes can grow up to 6.5 ft. (2 m) long. Their bite would make you feel unwell, but they're not deadly.

MONTJUÏC CASTLE

DELICIOSO!

Barcelona's food is a delicious mix of traditional dishes and new treats. Are you ready to tuck in?

START | CARRER DE LA FUSINA

CHOCOLATE HEAVEN

LA XOCOLATERIA BY ORIOL BALAGUER, CARRER DE LA FUSINA

Owned by master chocolatier (top chocolate chef) Oriol Balaguer, this store is filled with yummy treats. Balaguer has won numerous prizes for his sweet creations, including Best Dessert in the World in 2001. But many people just stop by for a delicious cup of hot chocolate, perfect when the weather gets colder in the city in wintertime.

ON DECEMBER 8, BARCELONA'S CHILDREN ARE GIVEN A HOLLOW LOG WITH A FACE, A RED HAT, AND ITS REAR END COVERED IN A CLOTH. IT'S CALLED A *CAGA TIÓ*, WHICH MEANS "POOP LOG"! THE CHILDREN LOOK AFTER THE LOG, FEEDING IT *TURRÓN* AND NUTS. THE MORE THEY FEED IT, THE MORE PRESENTS THEY HOPE TO SEE IT POOP OUT WHEN THEY HIT IT WITH A STICK ON DECEMBER 24!

TURRÓN TREAT

LA CAMPANA, CARRER DE LA PRINCESA

Turrón is a type of nougat candy made from sugar and almonds. It's usually eaten all over Spain at Christmas time. One of the most famous and best *turrón* stores in Barcelona is La Campana. It began serving locals their favorite Christmas candy over 120 years ago and is still going strong.

CARRER DE LA PRINCESA

BORN IN BARCELONA

PAPABUBBLE, CARRER AMPLE

Papabubble is a worldwide chain of candy stores now, but it was born in Barcelona in 2004. Visitors can watch the candy being made in front of them, and Papabubble is always experimenting to make new types of candy treats.

CARRER AMPLE

FROZEN FUN

ROCAMBOLESC, LA RAMBLA

There's a statue of explorer Christopher Columbus at the foot of La Rambla (see page 78). He's pointing out to sea, and in this fun ice-cream and popsicle store, you can buy a popsicle shaped like his famous pointing finger. There are also popsicles shaped like animals and even frozen noses!

CHUPA CHUPS LOLLIPOPS COME FROM BARCELONA! WHEN CANDY-MAKER ENRIC BERNAT SAW A CHILD GETTING STICKY HANDS WHILE EATING CANDY, IT GAVE HIM THE IDEA TO PUT CANDY ON A STICK, AND HE ASKED FAMOUS ARTIST SALVADOR DALI TO DESIGN THE WRAPPER. HIS WORLD-FAMOUS LOLLIPOP NAME COMES FROM THE SPANISH WORD CHUPAR, MEANING "TO SUCK."

17

CAKE CENTRAL

ESCRIBÀ PATISSERIE, LA RAMBLA

Barcelona has lots of delicious bakeries, and this is one of the oldest and most famous, providing cakes for the sweet-toothed for over 100 years. The outside of the building is covered in beautiful, sparkling mosaics. Inside, there are rows of tasty pastries and croissants with fillings such as banana and dark chocolate or mint and white chocolate. Yum!

LET'S GO TO MARKET

LA BOQUERIA, LA RAMBLA

La Boqueria is the oldest and most famous of Barcelona's food markets. It's a cavern of goodies, piled with juicy fruit, cheeses, sausages, and hams hanging on hooks. In the middle of the market, there's a large area of seafood stalls, selling everything from swordfish to sharks for dinner.

LA RAMBLA

SPANISH *JAMÓN* (HAM) IS WORLD FAMOUS FOR ITS DELICIOUS TASTE. YOU CAN BUY IT IN PAPER CONES AT THE MARKET TO NIBBLE ON AS A SNACK.

TAPAS-TASTIC
TICKETS BAR, AVENIDA PARALLEL

Tapas are small, savory snacks sold all over Spain, but the tapas bar owned by the superstar Catalan chefs Albert and Ferran Adrià is something special. They are world famous for their experimental food, so it's not surprising that their tapas are unusual and their restaurant is, too. It is like entering a circus, and visitors get to eat their dessert under a ceiling covered in giant model fruits. The unusual snacks that customers can buy have included cheese foam, liquid ravioli, and, for kids, there's a cotton candy tree – little clouds of cotton candy studded with fruit and served up on the branches of a bush.

AVENIDA PARALLEL

CHURROS HEAVEN
CARRER DE PETRITXOL

It's said that Spanish shepherds invented *churros*, little pieces of sweet dough that they cooked over open fires in the mountains. Their outdoor camping snack led to a never-to-be-forgotten treat called *chocolate con churros* – sugary, deep-fried dough sticks dipped in a pot of melted chocolate. This small, narrow street in the Gothic Quarter of the city is the place to find the best *churrerías* (*churros* stores), where the *churros* are freshly made before your very eyes. Thank you, shepherds of Spain!

search: LOCAL FOOD

TYPICAL BARCELONA DISHES TO TRY

MAR I MUNTANYA – This means "sea and mountain" and it refers to dishes that mix seafood and meat, such as paella.

MEL I MATÓ – Cream cheese drizzled with honey

BOTIFARRA AMB MONGETES – Sausage with white beans

CREMA CATALANA – A caramel custard topped with crunchy, melted sugar

ROMESCO SAUCE – Made with almonds, tomatoes, garlic, vinegar, and oil

IN SPAIN, PEOPLE DON'T USUALLY HAVE DINNER UNTIL BETWEEN 9 AND 10 P.M. CHILDREN OFTEN NAP IN THE AFTERNOON SO THEY CAN STAY UP LATE.

GAUDÍ TOWN

Antoni Gaudí is one of Barcelona's great artistic heroes. He designed some famous Barcelona buildings, a park, and an incredible cathedral that is still being finished. His work features dragons and sea monsters, magical forests, and seaweed. Follow in his footsteps to discover some of his secrets.

START

GÜELL PAVILIONS

CARRER DE BELLESGUARD

MOSAIC CASTLE

TORRE BELLESGUARD, CARRER DE BELLESGUARD

The site of this medieval-looking building was once a real castle belonging to a Barcelona king called Martin the Humane. Gaudí was inspired by the old castle when he built the new version, but he added his own style, too. He liked to decorate his buildings with bright mosaic pieces, called *trencadís*, and there are lots around the building, some on the very top of the high tower.

GAUDI COPIED NATURE ON HIS BUILDINGS, MAKING PARTS OF THEM LOOK LIKE NATURAL OBJECTS, SUCH AS SHELLS, SEAWEED, AND CORAL. HIS STYLE IS CALLED *MODERNISME*.

A DRAGON AT THE GATE

THE DRAGON GATE, GÜELL PAVILIONS

Gaudí loved using dragons in his work. This striking gateway he designed represents a mythical dragon guarding a magical garden – the Garden of the Hesperides – where golden apples grew. The dragon looks hungry, with his gaping mouth and forked tongue sticking out! In Greek mythology, his name is Ladon.

MEET THE MAN

THE GAUDÍ EXPERIENCE, CARRER DE LARRARD

Here you can put on a 4D headset and enter the virtual reality world of Gaudí, walking through the streets he knew and watching him work, or flying over the town like a bird to see his creations. Afterwards, you can even take a selfie next to his statue sitting on a bench.

PARK GÜELL

CARRER DE LARRARD

SIT ON A SERPENT

PARK GÜELL

Gaudí's park is like no other in the world. Visitors can walk through a forest of stone trees, and there's even a tiled bench shaped like a sea serpent, where people stop to get a great view over the town. There's also a fairytale caretaker's house and a giant lizard nicknamed El Drac (the dragon) at the entrance.

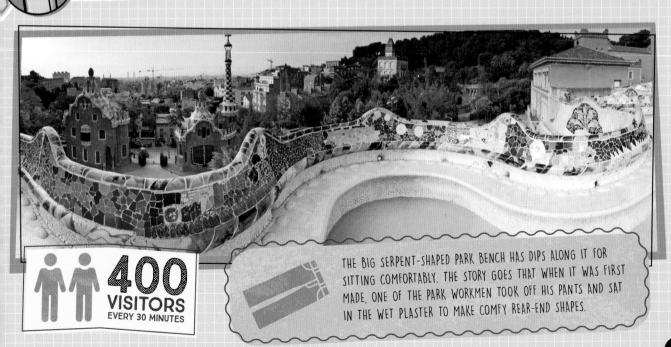

400 VISITORS
EVERY 30 MINUTES

THE BIG SERPENT-SHAPED PARK BENCH HAS DIPS ALONG IT FOR SITTING COMFORTABLY. THE STORY GOES THAT WHEN IT WAS FIRST MADE, ONE OF THE PARK WORKMEN TOOK OFF HIS PANTS AND SAT IN THE WET PLASTER TO MAKE COMFY REAR-END SHAPES.

BLESSED BUILDING SITE

SAGRADA FAMÍLIA, PLAÇA DE GAUDÍ

Gaudí's church, the Sagrada Família, is the most famous unfinished building in the world. It was begun in 1882, and architects are aiming to finish it in 2026, the 100th anniversary of Gaudí's death.

CHURCH OF CURVES

Gaudí wanted the basilica to celebrate the natural world, which he thought was created by God. There are no straight lines in the design because Gaudí said there were none in nature.

SAGRADA FAMÍLIA

FINAL HEIGHT
566 FT. / 172.5 M

PRESENT HEIGHT
443 FT. / 135 M

TOP BIRD SPOT

Gaudí used mountainsides as inspiration for the basilica walls, so he would probably be pleased that peregrine falcons, usually found nesting on high cliffs, build nests on the bell tower of the unfinished church every year. You can watch them and their chicks via a webcam.

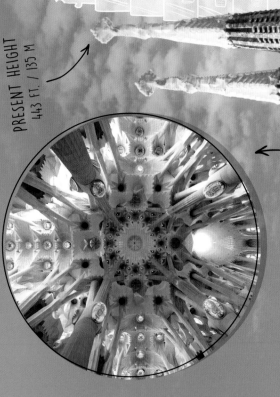

NATURE ALL AROUND

The nave of the church looks like a giant forest, and the ceiling is covered with leaves. All around the building there are animals to spot, such as snakes, lizards, snails, birds, and farm animals.

AFTER COMPLETION SAGRADA FAMÍLIA WILL HAVE:

18 TOWERS

13,000 PEOPLE CAPACITY

MAGIC MATH

On one of the walls outside the church, there's a square of numbers. When you add up the numbers horizontally or vertically, they total 33 – the age at which Jesus is said to have died.

1	14	14	4
11	7	6	9
8	10	10	5
13	2	3	15

SAGRADA OBSESSION

GAUDÍ BEGAN THE BASILICA PLANS AT AGE 31, AND IN HIS LATER YEARS, HE ENDED UP LIVING IN A SMALL HOUSE ON THE BUILDING SITE. HE EVENTUALLY GOT SO OBSESSED BY THE WORK THAT HE STOPPED LOOKING AFTER HIMSELF. HE HARDLY ATE AND HE DRESSED LIKE A HOMELESS PERSON, WEARING RAGGED SUITS AND SHOES MADE OF WOVEN PLANT ROOTS.

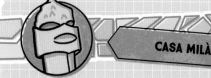
AHEAD OF THE CURVE

CASA MILÀ

When the Milà family asked Gaudí to build them a house, he created
a unique home that was completely curved, with no straight lines in it.
The house was soon given the nickname "The Quarry" because the front
of it looks like the rocky side of a quarry. On the roof there is a set of
chimneys that look like soldiers wearing ancient helmets.

THE HOUSE OF BONES

CASA BATLLÓ

This amazing Gaudí house is meant to be a dragon! Its roof
looks like a dragon's scaly back, and the balconies look like
bones, perhaps the dragon's victims! Inside, there is
a room called the Dragon's Belly, filled with arches that
make it look like the inside of a giant rib cage.

search: WHAT HAPPENED TO GAUDÍ?

TRAGIC TRAM ACCIDENT

Gaudí died at age 73. He was run over by a tram one day when he was out walking. He was so scruffy that people didn't recognize him when he was knocked down. They thought he was a homeless person.

PALAU GÜELL

MAGICAL ROOFTOPS

PALAU GÜELL

Gaudí is known for his crazy chimneys, and some of them are found on this home. They look like pieces of coral or fairytale candy, twisted and decorated with multicolored tiles.

GAUDÍ EXHIBITION CENTER

MODEL MAN

GAUDÍ EXHIBITION CENTER, MUSEU DIOCESÀ

Gaudí didn't like to make drawings of his designs. Instead, he made very detailed 3D models. His ideas were so complicated that modern architects have had to use computers to get the same effect. You can see models of his buildings here. Perhaps they will inspire you to make your own model building designs!

STREET SHOWS

Barcelona is a fantastic place to see street festivals and entertainment. The city loves to have fun outside. Follow the trail for some of the highlights.

PLAÇA D'ESPANYA

FRUITY FUN

PLAÇA D'ESPANYA

This is the main spot to celebrate Nit de cap d'any (New Year) in Barcelona. When the clock begins chiming at midnight, lots of people start to eat grapes – one for each chime – to bring good luck in the year ahead. The traditi... is called the *campanadas*. It's the reason that many peop... end up starting the New Year with a mouthful of grapes!

PARTY STREETS

FESTA MAJOR, PLAÇA DE LA VILA DE GRÀCIA

The *barrios* (districts) of Barcelona all have their own festivals. This August event is one big street party in the Gràcia part of town, going on for days. There's a competition for the best decorated street and lots of different events. *Gegants* (model giants) parade and dance, along with displays by *castellers* – people who climb up onto each other to make human pyramids (find out more on page 45). On the last evening, people dressed as fiery devils and dragons run through the streets.

ON NEW YEAR'S EVE, IT'S TIME TO KEEP A LOOKOUT FOR THE MYTHICAL *HOME DELS NASSOS*, THE MAN WITH 365 NOSES! LEGEND HAS IT THAT HE HAS ONE NOSE FOR EVERY DAY OF THE YEAR, BUT HE ONLY HAS ONE LEFT BY NEW YEAR'S EVE. THAT MAKES HIM IMPOSSIBLE TO FIND, OF COURSE, BUT LOTS OF YOUNG CHILDREN GET FOOLED INTO LOOKING BY THEIR PARENTS!

 START

PLAÇA DE LA VILA DE GRÀCIA

WATERY SHOW

MAGIC FOUNTAIN, PLAÇA DE CARLES BUÏGAS

The Magic Fountain provides a year-round outdoor street show. Its fountains rise and fall elegantly in time to music, and it can produce an incredible 7 billion different light and water combinations. Around 2.5 million visitors come to see its beautiful performances each year.

572 GALLONS (2,600 LITERS) OF WATER PER SECOND flow through the fountain's three pools.

LA RAMBLA

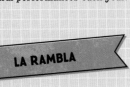

STONY FACES

HUMAN STATUES, LA RAMBLA

At the foot of La Rambla, the weekend crowds are usually joined by human street statues – actors who stand stock-still wearing incredible costumes, only occasionally making small moves as people throw coins into their boxes. They depict all kinds of characters. Some of them are funny, and some are people from myths and history.

THERE WERE ONCE SO MANY LIVING STATUES ON LA RAMBLA THAT THE ACTORS BEGAN TO GET INTO FIGHTS WITH EACH OTHER OVER THE BEST SPOTS TO STAND. EVENTUALLY, THE GOVERNMENT MADE THE STATUES APPLY FOR PERMITS AND NOW ONLY ALLOW A FEW EACH DAY.

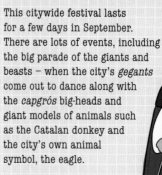

HERE COME THE GIANTS

LA MERCÉ FESTIVAL, PLAÇA DE SANT JAUME

This citywide festival lasts for a few days in September. There are lots of events, including the big parade of the giants and beasts – when the city's *gegants* come out to dance along with the *capgrós* big-heads and giant models of animals such as the Catalan donkey and the city's own animal symbol, the eagle.

FIERY NIGHTS

CORREFOC, CARRER FERRAN

Take cover if you see devils carrying fire and fire-breathing dragons running through the streets of Barcelona! They're taking part in a *correfoc*, or "fire run," a dramatic event that takes place at several street festivals. The biggest one is during the La Mercé Festival. The *diables* (devils) carry fireworks launchers and spray sparks everywhere. They even chase people in the crowd and throw firecrackers around. Obviously, don't try this at home!

CARRER FERRAN

search: PATRON SAINTS

SISTER OF MERCY

The La Mercé Festival is dedicated to Mary, Our Lady of Mercy. She is one of the Catholic patron saints of Barcelona and is credited with lots of miracles through the ages, when people prayed for her help and received it. She is said to have saved the city from invasions and even a plague of locusts.

LET THE PARTY BEGIN!

CARNIVAL, PASSEIG DEL BORN

The carnival fun starts in February, before the Christian festival of Lent begins. There are costume parades all over town, but the main procession features the arrival of the Carnival King and his ambassadors in horse-drawn carriages. The king is the lord of misrule and wild parties, and he announces the start of the fun. He's joined by Rodanxó and Rodanxona, *gegants* dressed in historical costume, who get the carnival dancing going.

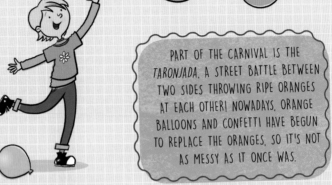

PART OF THE CARNIVAL IS THE *TARONJADA*, A STREET BATTLE BETWEEN TWO SIDES THROWING RIPE ORANGES AT EACH OTHER! NOWADAYS, ORANGE BALLOONS AND CONFETTI HAVE BEGUN TO REPLACE THE ORANGES, SO IT'S NOT AS MESSY AS IT ONCE WAS.

PASSEIG DEL BORN

NOVA ICÀRIA BEACH

IT'S LUCKY TO BURN SOMETHING ON THE NIT DE SANT JOAN, AND THERE ARE BONFIRES IN THE DISTRICTS ALL AROUND TOWN. PEOPLE BURN OLD FURNITURE IN THE FLAMES AND SOMETIMES THROW IN WISHES WRITTEN ON SLIPS OF PAPER.

BONFIRES AND A BEACH PARTY

NIT DE SANT JOAN, NOVA ICÀRIA BEACH

On the night of June 23, the Nit De Sant Joan, the streets are busy once again with a big celebration of Saint John the Baptist and also midsummer. Crowds head to the beach for a picnic dinner. There are lots of fireworks, and at midnight, everybody dives in for a good-luck swim.

WATERY WAY

Barcelona sits by the sparkling Mediterranean Sea. Take a walk along the shoreline to discover the sights and sounds of the city's life by the sea.

184 FT. (56 M) **LONG**
115 FT. (35 M) **HIGH**

START

BARCELONETA BEACH

DAYS OF SAND AND SUNSHINE

BARCELONETA BEACH

Barceloneta is Barcelona's beach neighborhood. There's always lots of fun going on, from skateboarding and beach volleyball to paddle boarding. All the way along there are *chiringuitos* (beach bars), perfect for a cooling drink or an ice cream.

BARCELONETA WASN'T ALWAYS A POPULAR BEACHFRONT. IT WAS ONCE A POOR SHANTY TOWN, RECLAIMED FROM BOGGY, SMELLY MUDFLATS. PIRATES USED TO LURK HERE, SPYING ON SHIPS AND PLOTTING ATTACKS.

A FISHY GIANT

FISH, BARCELONETA BEACH

Barcelona has its own giant goldfish. It's a sculpture called *Peix* (fish), by Frank Gehry, and it sits looking out over the sea, as if it's about to jump in for a swim. It's made of golden-colored stainless steel strips that look like scales when the sunlight reflects off them.

BARCELONETA BEACH

BARCELONETA HAS ITS OWN FLAG, WHICH YOU CAN SPOT FLYING AROUND THE AREA. IT HAS A SHIP AND A LIGHTHOUSE ON IT.

UNDERSEA GENIUS

STEAM-POWERED SUBMARINE, MOLL D'ESPANYA DEL PORT VELL

In 1862, a Barcelona inventor called Narcís Monturiol i Estarriol began experimenting in the harbor with the world's first engine-powered submarine. It was called *Ictíneo II*, and because Monturiol couldn't afford to build it with metal, he used olive wood. He made many successful dives around the harbor but he eventually ran out of money and his sub was sold for scrap. There's a replica of it down by the sea.

CANDY AND SINGING

FESTA MAJOR DE BARCELONETA, PLAÇA DE LA BARCELONETA

Barceloneta has its own festival at the end of September. There is a parade with fiery devils, *gegants*, and a big cannon that shoots candy at the crowd, fired by someone dressed as a historical general. Barceloneta's *gegants* are Pep Barceló, a giant fisherman, and Maria la Néta, who carries a basket of fish on her head.

PLAÇA DE LA BARCELONETA

SHHH... THE SHARKS ARE ASLEEP!

AQUARIUM, MOLL D'ESPANYA DEL PORT VELL

You can get up close to thousands of fish in Barcelona's aquarium. Its huge Oceanarium tank is home to scary-looking sharks and stingrays, as well as lots of smaller fish. The marine monsters can check out the visiting humans walking through a 262 ft. (80 m) long glass tunnel, but there's no need to worry – the sharks get hand-fed every day by the employees.

CHRISTMAS KINGS

CAVALCADA DE REIS, PORT VELL

Children in Barcelona get their Christmas presents on the night of January 5. That's when Los Reyes Magos, the Three Kings, arrive at the port by ship. Then they parade through town and the mayor gives them the key to Barcelona so that they can unlock every child's door and deliver lots of presents while everyone sleeps. Children leave out food and drinks for the kings and their camels, plus one of their shoes for the kings to fill with goodies.

BRAVE CHILDREN CAN HAVE A SLEEPOVER NEXT TO THE SHARKS IN THE AQUARIUM.

PORT VELL

SHIP AHOY

SANTA EULÀLIA SHIP, MOLL DE LA FUSTA

A beautiful old three-masted schooner, the *Santa Eulàlia*, sits on Barcelona's quay, reminding everyone of the city's great sea heritage. She used to deliver goods such as grain and wood around the Mediterranean, and she was once used for smuggling. She didn't smuggle rum or treasure, though. She smuggled flour, hidden from officials who wanted to tax her owners for their cargo. Now the city's Maritime Museum looks after her (see page 34).

A CITY BY THE WAVES

SIGHTSEEING BOATS, MOLL DE LES DRASSANES

You can take a sightseeing boat around the harbor, which would once have been filled with ships. You would have seen Ancient Roman galleys here, being loaded with popular Catalan goods – stone blocks, wine, and fish paste – to take back to Rome. Later, the port was built, and Barcelona would have seen many ships come and go. Some of them came to grief in Mediterranean storms, and there are lots of shipwrecks off the coast.

WHEN BUILDERS BEGAN WORK ON A NEW BARCELONETA APARTMENT BLOCK, THEY DUG UP A SHIPWRECK FROM AROUND 800 YEARS AGO. THE SITE OF THE OLD WOODEN WRECK WOULD ONCE HAVE BEEN UNDERWATER.

ROW TO VICTORY OR DIE

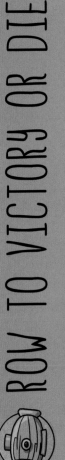

MARITIME MUSEUM

Barcelona's Maritime Museum is built in the Royal Shipyards. They date from the 13th century, making them among the most complete medieval dockyards in the world. The museum is full of models and mementos, plus a replica of a famous ship, a galley that was powered by rowers. It was rowed into battle by slaves in chains.

MARITIME MUSEUM

SHIP-SHAPE AGAIN

This is a replica of *Real*, the royal galley of Don Juan of Austria. In 1571, it helped to win victory over the Turks at the Battle of Lepanto. The original galley would have been built in the shipyards, and the replica was built to commemorate the battle 400 years later.

LANTERNS

THE *REAL'S* STERN WAS COVERED IN ORNATE SCULPTURES AND PAINTINGS.

THE GALLEY IS PAINTED RED AND GOLD — THE TRADITIONAL ROYAL COLORS OF SPAIN.

197 FT. (60 M) LONG

20 FT. (6.2 M) WIDE

290 OARSMEN PER BOAT

THE BOW HAD A RAM, GRAPPLING HOOKS, AND CATAPULTS FOR FIGHTING OTHER SHIPS.

...SAT ON THESE OUTER EDGES.

ALL ABOARD

Both sides mainly used slaves to power their galleys. For instance, the Turks had around 37,000 oarsmen, many of them enemy prisoners. As well as the oarsmen there were sailors and soldiers on board each galley. Around 150,000 people took part in the battle overall. After the battle, the victorious side set around 12,000 slaves free from the losing ships and took about 10,000 Turks prisoner.

AWFUL OARS

GALLEYS WERE ROWED BY SLAVES, CONVICTED CRIMINALS, OR PRISONERS-OF-WAR, WHO WERE CHAINED TO THEIR SEATS BELOW DECK. THERE, THEY HAD TO SLEEP, EAT, AND GO TO THE BATHROOM. OFTEN FOR A WEEK AT A TIME BETWEEN PORTS. THREE TO FIVE MEN WOULD HAVE BEEN SQUASHED TOGETHER MANNING EACH OAR IN THE STINKING HEAT. THE *REAL* HAD 290 ROWERS.

FIERCE FIGHTING

The battle was fought between Spanish and Venetian forces, led by Don Juan, and an Ottoman (Turkish) fleet. It was the last big battle ever to be fought between boats powered by rowers. For an hour during the battle, the crew of the *Real* fought the crew of the galley *Sultana*, commanded by the Ottoman leader Ali Pasha. Eventually, Ali Pasha was killed and beheaded. His head was stuck on a spike for all to see, and when the Turkish fleet saw it, they knew they were beaten.

LET'S GO!

How would you like to travel around Barcelona – by cable car, train, tram, bicycle, or perhaps even skateboard? Hop on board the travel trail...

A CAR THAT FLOATS

MONTJUÏC CABLE CAR

There are two cable cars in Barcelona, perfect for getting a bird's-eye view of town. One crosses the harbor, with a great view of the ships below, and the other is the Montjuïc Cable Car, which runs up to Montjuïc Castle (see page 15) and saves visitors the climb to the park at the top of the hill.

2,467 FT. (752 M) **LONG**
CABLE CAR TO MONTJUÏC

558 FT. (170 M) **HIGH**
TO MONTJUÏC CASTLE

START

TELEFÈRIC DE MONTJUÏC

SKATEBOARD CENTRAL

SKATEBOARDERS, PLAÇA DELS ÀNGELS

This is the spot where Barcelona's skateboarders like to hang out and practice tricks, and it's a great place to watch them. The architects of the nearby Museum of Contemporary Art handily lef smooth granite ledges and steps here tha are perfect for grinds, flips, and airs.

PLAÇA DELS ÀNGELS

WHEELY GOOD FUN
PASSEIG DE LLUÍS COMPANYS

Barcelona is a cycle-friendly city, with lots of bike paths. The wide thoroughfare that runs down towards Ciutadella Park is a popular spot for cycling and cycle tours. It's a good place to rent bikes to cycle around the park. You can rent four-person bicycles here, so all the family can ride together. And if you're tired and want someone else to do the pedaling, you can even travel in a Trixi – it's part bike, part taxi!

BARCELONA IS IN THE TOP 20 MOST BICYCLE-FRIENDLY CITIES IN THE WORLD, ACCORDING TO THE BICYCLE-FRIENDLY CITIES INDEX, COMPILED EACH YEAR.

KEEP AN EYE OUT FOR TRIXIS, PEDAL-POWERED TAXIS IN THE WATERFRONT AREA OF BARCELONA.

URQUINAONA STATION

AROUND TOWN UNDERGROUND
URQUINAONA STATION

The Barcelona Metro runs under the city. It has 180 stations, but there are also several "ghost stations" – the name for abandoned stations that were built but closed or never used. Who knows if ghosts actually get on and off there! Opened in 1926, Urquinaona is the only working station that still has its original ironwork entrance, located on Carrer del Bruc. Gaudí himself might have walked under its curly sign.

OLD-TIMERS ON THE TRACKS

TRAMVIA BLAU

There are lots of modern trams running through the city, but the oldest of all is the Tramvia Blau, dating all the way back to 1901. It takes visitors up Avinguda del Tibidabo, passing lots of grand mansions, to the foot of Mount Tibidabo.

THE CITY'S FIRST-EVER TRAMS WERE PULLED BY HORSES. THEN, THEY BECAME STEAM-POWERED. NOW, THEY RUN ON ELECTRICITY.

CABLE MOUNTAIN

TIBIDABO FUNICULAR

Funicular railways are carriages that move up and down hills on cables. You can take funicular rides up to Montjuïc and to the Collserola Natural Park, but the oldest one in Barcelona chugs up the steep hill to the Tibidabo Amusement Park. People have been boarding since 1901, which is over 100 years of funicular fun.

TIBIDABO FUNICULAR

25%

TAKING IT OFF-ROAD

COLLSEROLA NATURAL PARK

The wooded valleys and forest paths of Barcelona's Collserola Natural Park make for good mountain-biking country. The riders get amazing views of the city and also get to see all kinds of interesting animals, such as birds of prey, tree frogs, and even wild boar! For people who like to power themselves, it's excellent walking country, too.

TIBIDABO AMUSEMENT PARK

FLYING HIGH

THE AVIÓ RIDE, TIBIDABO AMUSEMENT PARK

The Avió (airplane) ride is a famous fairground attraction that flies over the Tibidabo mountaintop, with a fantastic view of the city below. It is a replica of the first aircraft to fly from Barcelona to Madrid, in 1927, and it's been going around and around, powered by its own propeller, since 1928. Barcelona's oldest *avis* or *abuelos* (Catalan and Spanish words for "grandparents") may have ridden it when they were children!

COLLSEROLA NATURAL PARK

WINNING CITY

Barcelona has one of the world's best-known soccer teams, but did you know that it also has some of the world's best competitive human-castle builders? On your mark for the sports trail. Get set. Go!

SOCCER CITY

CAMP NOU

FC Barcelona is one of the world's best soccer clubs, so it's not surprising that the city is soccer-mad. The team is nicknamed Barça, and it's based in the famous Camp Nou, the biggest stadium in Europe.

THE NAME CAMP NOU MEANS "NEW STADIUM" BUT IT WAS FIRST OPENED IN 1957. THE CLUB ITSELF WAS FOUNDED IN 1899 BY A SWISS SOCCER FAN.

CAMP NOU

99,354
CROWD CAPACITY

Barcelona won a world-record six major soccer trophies in the 2008–2009 season.

SPOT THE SHIRTS

F C B

Barcelona plays in dark red and blue. Its supporters call the colors the *blaugrana*. The club's motto, *Més que un club*, means "more than a club." The club crest shows the Catalan flag, the cross of Saint George, the team colors, and a soccer ball.

SING FOR BARÇA

The club anthem is usually sung at matches. Here's an English translation of some of the words:

"We all agree! We all agree! One flag seals our brotherhood: Blue and claret in the wind. Our cry is bold. We have a name That everybody knows. Barça! Barça! Barça!"

THE BIG MATCH

Every year, Barcelona plays their big rival, Real Madrid. The game is called El Clásico and is watched all over the world. It's one of the most watched soccer games in the world, along with the Champion's League Final.

THE TEAM IS FAMOUS FOR PLAYING TIKI-TAKA, A STYLE OF SOCCER WHEN THE PLAYERS MAKE LOTS OF VERY ACCURATE PASSES TO EACH OTHER.

TOP TRAINING

LA MASIA IS THE CLUB'S SOCCER ACADEMY, WHERE YOUNG PEOPLE TRAIN TO PLAY BARCELONA-STYLE. WORLD-FAMOUS PLAYERS SUCH AS LIONEL MESSI LEARNED THE GAME HERE. HE HAS WON THE WORLD SOCCER PLAYER OF THE YEAR AWARD A RECORD FIVE TIMES — THE SAME AS REAL MADRID'S CRISTIANO RONALDO.

INDOOR ACTION

PALAU BLAUGRANA

The Palau Blaugrana indoor arena belongs to FC Barcelona and it's located on the same site as the Camp Nou stadium. It's home to Barcelona's popular basketball team, as well as handball, roller hockey, and *futsal* teams (*futsal* is a version of five-a-side soccer).

AT THE BARCELONA OLYMPICS IN 1992, THE US FAMOUSLY SENT THEIR BASKETBALL "DREAM TEAM" OF CELEBRITY PLAYERS, SUCH AS MICHAEL JORDAN AND MAGIC JOHNSON. THEY WON THE GOLD MEDAL EASILY, AND THE TEAM WAS SO FULL OF STARS THAT IT'S OFTEN DESCRIBED AS THE BEST TEAM EVER TO COMPETE IN ANY SPORT.

PALAU BLAUGRANA

CAN YOU BEAT THE BEST?

OLYMPIC MUSEUM

The 1992 Barcelona Olympics were a huge success. Millions watched on TV as the world's best athletes competed. At Barcelona's Olympic Museum, you can find out all about Olympic competitions and use simulators to compete against some of the world's best sportspeople of all time.

OLYMPIC MUSEUM

search: BARCELONA OLYMPICS

📍 11 YEARS OLD
The youngest competitor in the 1992 games was Spaniard Carlos Front, a coxswain in a rowing eight. He was only 11 years old!

📍 MEDAL RECORD
Belarus gymnast Vitaly Scherbo won six gold medals at the Barcelona Olympics, four of them on the same day. That's a world record for the number of Olympic golds in one day.

📍 9,356
The total number of athletes who competed in the games

CYCLING SUPERSTARS

MONTJUÏC

OLYMPIC PARK

In March, some of the world's best road cyclists come to Catalonia to compete in the Volta a Catalunya, a grueling seven-day race through the countryside. They must ride up brutally steep mountains and try to win super-fast sprints before ending their race on an eight-lap ride around Montjuïc in Barcelona. The overall winner is awarded a prestigious white-and-green cycling jersey.

THIS SHIP FROM THE OPENING CEREMONY REPRESENTS MEDITERRANEAN CULTURE.

MONTJUÏC

IMAGINE THE MOMENT

OLYMPIC PARK

You can go inside Barcelona's Olympic Stadium to experience the place where so many medals were won or lost. Cobi the Catalan sheepdog was the 1992 Olympic mascot, and you can see a bronze statue of Cobi in the Vila Olímpica.

HANG ON TO WIN

PLAÇA NOVA

During festivals, you might see a traditional Catalan sport played on a *cucaña*, a greasy pole that competitors must climb. The oldest and best preserved *cucaña* in Catalonia can be seen at the Festival of Sant Roc on Plaça Nova on August 16. It is slightly different from other *cucañas* as it is not greased and it's horizontal instead of vertical. But that doesn't make it any easier, because it spins around, making it very hard to stay on.

PLAÇA NOVA

LA RAMBLA

WE WON

CANALETAS FOUNTAIN, LA RAMBLA

Barcelona soccer fans come to celebrate wins here. They've been doing it since the 1930s, when the soccer scores used to be written on a blackboard by the fountain for everyone to see. Legend says that if you drink from the Canaletas Fountain before leaving the city, you will return to Barcelona.

PYRAMIDS OF PEOPLE
PLAÇA DE SANT MIQUEL

Castellers are teams of people who climb on each other's shoulders to make human towers. There are castle-building societies all over Catalonia, and the Barcelona *castellers* are among the best. The teams are judged in competitions against each other for the highest, most complicated towers. The famous *castellers* of the city are celebrated with a sculpture in Plaça de Sant Miquel, and they perform at festivals around town, especially during La Mercé (see page 28) and the Gràcia Festival.

(see page 28)

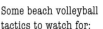

PLAÇA DE SANT MIQUEL

THE STRONGEST *CASTELLERS* ARE AT THE BOTTOM. THEN COMES THE TRUNK, AND THEN THE CROWN. A CHILD, THE *ENXANETA*, CLIMBS TO THE VERY TOP AND LIFTS HIS OR HER HANDS TO SIGNIFY THE CROWNING OF THE CASTLE.

EACH *CASTELLER* TEAM HAS A CAPTAIN, WHO DIRECTS EVERYONE BUILDING THE CASTLE AND THEN TAKING IT DOWN SAFELY. WHILE THE CASTLE IS BEING BUILT, MUSICIANS PLAY ON PIPES AND DRUMS.

BOGATELL BEACH

SPIKING, ROLLING, AND DINKING
BOGATELL AND OTHER BEACHES

Beach volleyball is a popular sport on the beaches of Barcelona. There are many nets around Bogatell Beach, and international beach volleyball tournaments are sometimes held at Port Olimpic.

Some beach volleyball tactics to watch for:

SPIKING – hitting the ball with an open hand, slamming it down from above the top of the net

ROLLING – similar to spiking but hitting the ball more softly and in more of an arc

DINKING – tapping the ball softly, low over the net

MUSICAL MARVELS

Barcelona pulses to the beat of a multitude of music festivals every year. Dance your way along this trail to discover unusual instruments, powerful street folk dances, and one of the best young music scenes in Europe.

2,400+

NUMBER OF MUSICAL INSTRUMENTS OWNED BY THE MUSEUM

START

PARC DEL FÒRUM

HOUSE OF MUSIC

MUSIC MUSEUM

The city's music museum houses different musical instruments from all around the world, including some very unusual and rare ones. Can you guess how to play a claviorganum, for instance? Would you blow it, strum it, or play its keys? See the side of the page to find out! The museum also has one of the best guitar collections on the planet, and visitors can have a go at playing real musical instruments such as an electric guitar, a harp, or a cello.

HERE ARE SOME OF THE TRADITIONAL CATALAN INSTRUMENTS TO LOOK OUT FOR IN THE MUSEUM AND AT BARCELONA FESTIVALS:

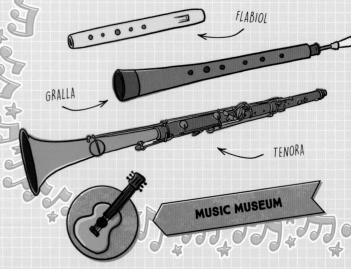

FLABIOL

GRALLA

TENORA

MUSIC MUSEUM

BEST SOUND AROUND

PRIMAVERA SOUND, PARC DEL FÒRUM

The name of Barcelona's super-cool music festival translates as "spring sound." It happens around the end of May each year, with performances from the world's top bands and solo artists. It showcases new, young musicians, too, so it's a good place to spot future superstars.

DANCE OF PRIDE

SARDANA DANCE, PLAÇITA DE LA SEU

Locals usually head to the square in front of the cathedral on Sunday mornings to dance the *sardana*. They hold hands in a circle while making intricate steps with their feet, and anyone can join in provided they know the moves. The dance is accompanied by a live band called a *cobla*, which is made up of Catalan brass instruments, flutes, and tambourines.

THE *SARDANA* DANCE IS A SYMBOL OF CATALONIA. BETWEEN 1936 AND 1939, SPAIN WAS SPLIT BY A CIVIL WAR FOUGHT BETWEEN THE NATIONALISTS AND REPUBLICANS. EVENTUALLY, BARCELONA FELL TO THE NATIONALISTS, AND GENERAL FRANCO TOOK CONTROL OF SPAIN. HE BANNED THE CATALAN LANGUAGE AND CUSTOMS, INCLUDING THE *SARDANA* DANCE, BUT THE BAN HAD THE OPPOSITE EFFECT TO WHAT HE WANTED. THE DANCE CAME TO REPRESENT PEOPLE'S PRIDE IN BEING CATALAN.

PALACE OF LIGHT

PALAU DE LA MÚSICA CATALANA

you translate this concert hall's name, it eans the "palace of music," and it really does ok like a musical monarch's crazy, beautiful alace. It was built over 100 years ago and has credible glass ceilings. When people play here uring the day, they are bathed in the light at pours in through the stained glass.

PALAU DE LA MÚSICA CATALANA

47

CONCERT CORNER

CORNER OF CARRER DEL BISBE AND CARRER DE LA PIETAT

You can see buskers all over Barcelona, but this particular corner, on a small street behind the cathedral, is reserved for the best buskers of all. It's a chance for passersby to hear some of the most beautiful music in the city outside a concert hall. The musicians who play here always draw large crowds.

THE LICEU

THE SONGS GO ON

THE LICEU

The city's stunning horseshoe-shaped opera house has had an eventful history. It's almost been destroyed several times: twice by major fires and once by a bomb explosion. Legend says it was built over the remains of a medieval execution site, and some have even suggested that it could be cursed and haunted!

BARCELONA'S MOST FAMOUS OPERA SINGER IS MONTSERRAT CABALLÉ, WHO BECAME WORLD RENOWNED FOR HER SOPRANO VOICE. LOOK FOR HER DUET WITH QUEEN'S FREDDIE MERCURY. THE TWO HAD A HUGE HIT WHEN THEY SANG THE SONG "BARCELONA" TOGETHER, AND IT BECAME A MUSICAL SYMBOL OF THE 1992 BARCELONA OLYMPICS.

EVERYBODY DANCE!

CASA DE LA DANSA

This "house of dance" is where some of the city's best dancers perform. As soon as they can walk, the children of Barcelona can join in the fun dance activities that happen here.

search: BARCELONA BEATS

SOUNDS OF THE CITY

Barcelona has a big modern music scene. Lots of rock bands and folk musicians base themselves in the city. Keep an ear out for Barcelona's own Catalan rumba style of music, which combines Cuban and flamenco sounds with a modern beat.

FLAMENCO IS THE PASSIONATE, FOOT-STOMPING DANCE OF SPAIN, CLOSELY ASSOCIATED WITH THE COUNTRY'S ROMANI PEOPLE. BARCELONA DANCER CARMEN AMAYA IS SAID TO HAVE BEEN THE GREATEST FLAMENCO DANCER EVER. SHE WAS BORN IN A SHANTYTOWN NEAR THE SEAFRONT JUST OVER 100 YEARS AGO AND BEGAN DANCING WHEN SHE WAS SIX. SHE SAID THAT SHE LEARNED TO DANCE TO THE RHYTHMS OF THE WAVES THAT LAPPED THE BARCELONA SHORE.

SÓNAR FESTIVAL

MEGA MUSIC PARTY

SÓNAR FESTIVAL

Barcelona's big electronic music festival happens in mid-June, attracting DJs and bands from around the world. Thousands of music fans from all over Europe arrive in the city to enjoy the latest tracks played live.

CASA DE LA DANSA

PERFECT PARKS

Take a relaxing trip through Barcelona's parks to meet a few goddesses,
a water cat, a giant claw, and, of course, some dragons!

WATCHED OVER BY GODDESSES

CIUTADELLA PARK

This big park is a green oasis right in the middle of town. It's a great place to go boating, munch on a picnic, or see some unusual creatures.

CIUTADELLA PARK

READY FOR RAIN

The *Lady of the Umbrella* stands at the entrance to Barcelona Zoo in the park. She was sculpted to mark a big exhibit held in the park over 100 years ago, and she's wearing clothes from the time. She looks as if she is holding out her hand to see if it has stopped raining.

THE LAKE OF GODDESSES

You can row around the boating lake under the eyes of two Ancient Roman goddesses on the beautiful park waterfall. On top of the waterfall, Aurora, the goddess of dawn, is riding in her chariot pulled by golden horses. Venus, the goddess of love, is standing in a seashell, as if she's about to dive in for a swim.

CIRCUS SPOT

The park is a good place to see performers practicing circus skills such as tightrope walking and juggling. Drummers and guitarists play in the park, too.

RORA

VENUS

TWO STONE TRICKSTERS

THE PARK IS FULL OF STATUES OF FAMOUS PEOPLE, BUT THERE ARE ALSO TWO CHARACTERS FROM AN OLD STORY. A STONE STORK AND FOX SIT ON A FOUNTAIN, REPRESENTING A TALE ABOUT A FOX INVITING HIS FRIEND THE STORK FOR A MEAL. HE SERVED SOUP IN A BOWL, WHICH HE COULD LAP UP BUT THE STORK COULD NOT. IN RETURN, THE STORK INVITED THE FOX FOR A MEAL AND SERVED THE FOOD IN A JAR WITH A NARROW NECK. THE STORK COULD GET HIS BEAK INSIDE BUT THE FOX COULDN'T REACH ANYTHING, SO THE TRICKSTER FOUND HIMSELF TRICKED.

75 ACRES (30 HECTARES)

100+ WILD BIRD SPECIES

ZOO IMPOSTERS

Barcelona's zoo is over a hundred years old and has all sorts of animals, from crocodiles to tigers. Outside the zoo, there are lots of wild birds, including a colony of elegant gray herons. They stalk around inside the zoo, finding food meant for the captive birds, so people think the herons live there.

THE SONG OF THE CAT

LARIBAL GARDENS

This peaceful garden is on the slopes of Montjuïc. It's famous for the Font del Gat (fountain of the cat). Water has been flowing out of this cat's mouth on and off for a century, and it has its own famous children's song, "Baixant de la Font del Gat" (down by the cat fountain), about a young woman who meets her true love at the fountain. You can listen to it and learn the lyrics online.

1,350 DIFFERENT SPECIES IN THE GARDEN

BARCELONA BOTANICAL GARDENS

SMELL THE WORLD

BARCELONA BOTANICAL GARDENS

This is a good place to pretend you're on a world adventure. There are plants from all over the world, including specimens from Australia, South Africa, and California. Some of the tallest trees in the city can be found here, too. There's even a sensory garden designed for you to smell and touch.

LARIBAL GARDENS

search: PARK SIZES IN BARCELONA

📍 **21,000 ACRES** (8,460 HECTARES)
Collserola Natural Park

📍 **76 ACRES** (31 HECTARES)
Ciutadella Park

PETAL PRIZES

CERVANTES PARK

The city's huge rose garden has around 245 varieties – everything from the world's most fragrant to the largest and the smallest type of rose. There are even blue roses. Each year, the park hosts the International New Rose Competition, and contestants come from around the globe hoping to win a prize for their blooms. The winning rose is planted in the park, a great honor if you are a rose grower.

10,000 ROSE BUSHES IN THE PARK

ORENETA PARK

ALL ABOARD FOR THE CASTLE

ORENETA PARK

The remains of Oreneta Castle give this park its name – *oreneta* means "swallow" in Catalan. The park is famous for its miniature train ride, said to be one of the best in Europe. The tiny train line has its own station and staff, and trundles around the park, through tunnels and over bridges, for 2,087 ft. (636 m).

A GIANT CLAW
CREUETA DEL COLL PARK

This park has a great public pool, but also a weird and striking sculpture – Eduardo Chillida's *In Praise of Water*. It's a massive concrete claw suspended by huge metal cables. The artist hoped his work would remind people of the vastness of the universe.

CREUETA DEL COLL PARK

HORTA'S LABYRINTH PARK

"Where are you?"

"I'm lost!"

AMAZING MAZE
HORTA'S LABYRINTH PARK

This is the oldest park in Barcelona, and it has a fantastic maze of high hedges. It invites visitors to reenact the story of the ancient hero Theseus, who entered a maze to fight the Minotaur, a half-bull and half-human monster that ate people! Luckily, all you will find in the middle of this maze is a statue of Eros, the Greek god of love.

TIBIDABO

MAGIC MOUNTAIN

TIBIDABO AMUSEMENT PARK

Where would you find a mysterious castle, a square of dreams, and a hall of crazy mirrors? They're all attractions at the top of Mount Tibidabo, where Barcelona's 100-year-old amusement park is still a big hit with everyone. Highlights include the plane ride that flies out over the city (see page 39), the rollercoaster that speeds through the forest at 50 mph (80 kph), an aerial railway, and a colorful big wheel. There's a virtual reality ride, too.

THE AMUSEMENT PARK FIRST OPENED IN 1901, WHEN CROWDS WERE THRILLED BY THE AMAZING NEW INVENTIONS ON SHOW, SUCH AS POSTCARD VENDING MACHINES AND BINOCULARS.

COUNTRYSIDE IN THE CITY

COLLSEROLA NATURAL PARK

Sitting high above Barcelona, this huge stretch of countryside is one of the biggest city parks in the world. It has hiking and biking trails (see page 39) and lots of wildlife. Birdwatchers come from all over the world to see the birds of prey that live here, especially when they migrate in the fall. You can see birds such as peregrines, ospreys, and short-toed eagles when they set off on their winter migration journeys.

COLLSEROLA NATURAL PARK

SHORT—TOED EAGLE

43 SQ MI
(111 SQ KM)
THE SIZE OF THE PARK

55

CITY OF ART

Get some inspiration for your own creations by strolling around town in the footsteps of famous artists and talented craftspeople.

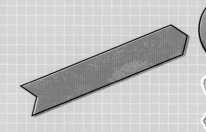

BARCELONA BORN

JOAN MIRÓ FOUNDATION

Joan Miró was born in Barcelona and began attending drawing classes in the city when he was just seven years old. He went on to become a world-famous 20th-century artist. Every day, thousands of people walk over his mosaic on La Rambla or sit by his sculptures in the Joan Miró Park. He has his own Barcelona museum, too.

MIRÓ DIDN'T REPRESENT THINGS REALISTICALLY. HE TRANSFORMED THEM INTO A GROUP OF SHAPES TO REPRESENT PEOPLE, ANIMALS, THE STARS, OR THE MOON. HE USED BRIGHT COLORS SUCH AS RED, BLUE, AND YELLOW. MIRÓ SAID HE WANTED TO DESTROY THE IDEA OF REALISTIC PAINTING.

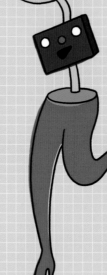

CURRENT CRAFT

POBLE ESPANYOL

Visitors can see all kinds of crafts being made at the Poble Espanyol, an open-air museum of Spanish streets and buildings. Glassblowers, jewelry-makers, and weavers have their workshops here, using craft skills that have been passed down over the centuries.

START

JOAN MIRÓ FOUNDATION

THE ARTIST WHO USED EVERYTHING

ANTONI TÀPIES FOUNDATION

Antoni Tàpies was a Barcelona-born artist who became world famous in the 1960s and 1970s. He added all kinds of unusual things to his paintings, including clay dust, wastepaper, rags, and string, to represent the "matter" the world is made of. Artists all over the world were influenced by his exciting style.

ANTONI TÀPIES SET UP AN ART FOUNDATION IN BARCELONA WHERE YOU CAN SEE HIS WORK. HE DECORATED THE BUILDING WITH A GIANT METAL SCULPTURE CALLED *NÚVOL I CADIRA*, WHICH MEANS "CLOUD AND CHAIR." IT SHOWS A CHAIR ON TOP OF A HUGE CLOUD AND IS OPEN TO INTERPRETATION. WHAT DO YOU THINK IT MEANS?

ART FOR ALL

CRAFT MARKET, PLAÇA DE SANT JOSEP ORIOL

You can buy your own Barcelona paintings from artists who sell their work at street markets in and around the city center. On La Rambla, you can sometimes sit down and have your portrait painted by a super-quick portrait artist.

EVERYONE INVOLVED

THE KISS MURAL,
PLAÇA D'ISIDRE NONELL

This famous mural looks like two people kissing, but move in closer and you'll see that it's made up of hundreds of tiny photos printed on tiles. The artist, Joan Fontcuberta, asked people to send him their photos representing what freedom means to them. Then he used the photos to create the mural. It's called *El Món Neix en Cada Besada*, which means "the world is born with every kiss." It represents personal freedom.

4,000 PHOTOS IN MURAL

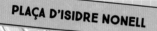
PLAÇA D'ISIDRE NONELL

PICASSO MUSEUM

GENIUS IN TOWN

PICASSO MUSEUM

Pablo Picasso became one of the best-known artists in the world in the 20th century. He began his career in Barcelona when he moved to the city, aged only 13, and started sketching the people and places he saw. Some of his early work is on show in a Barcelona museum dedicated to him.

EVENTUALLY, PICASSO BECAME KNOWN FOR PAINTING IN A STYLE CALLED CUBISM. HIS CUBIST PICTURES SHOW THINGS BROKEN UP INTO SHAPES AND REARRANGED. HE SAID HE PAINTED THINGS AS HE THOUGHT OF THEM, NOT AS HE SAW THEM.

PICASSO'S WORLD-FAMOUS SIGNATURE IS VERY VALUABLE. SOMETIMES THE GREAT ARTIST REFUSED TO SIGN HIS OWN PAINTINGS. HE EVEN SAID ONE OF HIS OWN PAINTINGS WAS FAKE! WHEN PICASSO'S FRIEND TOLD HIM THAT HE HAD ACTUALLY SEEN HIM PAINTING IT, PICASSO SAID, "I CAN PAINT FALSE PICASSOS JUST AS WELL AS ANYBODY."

MAKERS LIVED HERE

EL BORN NEIGHBORHOOD

This old part of town was once full of craftspeople busy making things. Some of the street names will tell you what was made there. Carrer de l'Argenteria means "silversmiths' street." Carrer dels Mirallers means "mirror-makers' street." Carrer dels Sombrerers means "hat-makers' street."

CARRER DELS SOMBRERERS

WONDROUS WALL ART

ALL OVER BARCELONA

There is lots of wall art around town, including a big wall at the back of Barcelona Zoo reserved for great street graffiti. A huge skull, a giant hand, a big bicycle wheel, and a floating building are a few of the amazing images that have been created here.

search: YOUNG PICASSO

CHILD'S PLAY

Apparently, Picasso's first word was *piz*, which is short for "pencil" in Spanish. His dad was an artist and art professor who started teaching him when he was seven. He got into quite a lot of trouble at school because he didn't like being told what to do. But he didn't mind detention because it gave him the chance to sketch quietly for hours.

ALL OVER BARCELONA

HIGH TIME

Barcelona has some spectacular hilltop views, a hi-tech skyscraper that changes color, some monsters living on its rooftops, and one of the most famous swimming-pool views on the planet. Welcome to the highest trail in town!

945 FT. (288 M) HIGH

SEE RIGHT AROUND TOWN
TORRE DE COLLSEROLA

This huge telecommunications and radio tower is in Collserola Natural Park. It's the tallest building in town, and it broadcasts the city's TV and radio signals.

START

TIBIDABO

TORRE DE COLLSEROLA

SEEING FROM THE SKY
TEMPLE DEL SAGRAT COR, TIBIDABO

Way up above Barcelona, Jesus stands with his arms outstretched on top of this church, looking out over the city from Mount Tibidabo. Visitors can go up and up, via stairs and elevators, to see the amazing view.

VISITORS WHO AREN'T SCARED OF HEIGHTS CAN GO TO THE 10TH OF ITS 13 FLOORS TO SEE THE 360-DEGREE VIEW OF BARCELONA.

TIBADABO MEANS "I WILL GIVE TO YOU." IT COMES FROM A LEGEND THAT THE DEVIL BROUGHT JESUS TO THE TOP OF THE HILL AND TRIED TO TEMPT HIM BY SHOWING HIM THE VIEWS. HE SAID, "HAEC TIBI OMNIA DABO SI CADENS ADORAVERIS ME," WHICH IS LATIN FOR, "ALL THIS I WILL GIVE TO YOU, IF YOU KNEEL AND WORSHIP ME." JESUS'S STATUE, WATCHING OVER THE CITY, SYMBOLIZES HIS REFUSAL TO LISTEN TO THE DEVIL.

AS FAR AS YOU CAN GO

PLANETARIUM AT COSMOCAIXA

You can travel into space and learn about the universe at this planetarium, using 3D technology. Visitors can wear stereoscopic glasses and sit inside a dome to experience what it would be like to travel in deep space!

COSMOCAIXA

THE CARMEL BUNKERS

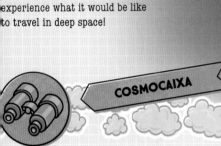

VIEW OF WAR

THE CARMEL BUNKERS

These old Spanish Civil War bunkers are located on top of a hill in Guindardó Park. They used to house anti-aircraft guns. Today, they offer one of the best views over the city. In the evening, people gather here to sing songs and watch the sun set.

AFTER THE SPANISH CIVIL WAR, MANY IN THE CITY WERE LEFT HOMELESS. IN THE 1940S AND 1950S, THE BUNKERS PROVIDED SHELTER. THEY BECAME PART OF A SHANTYTOWN FOR AROUND 3,000 PEOPLE. THERE IS A SMALL MUSEUM INSIDE THE BUNKERS TELLING THEIR UNUSUAL STORY.

HIGH-TECH

TORRE AGBAR

This cucumber-shaped skyscraper constantly changes color. It is covered in multicolored aluminum, which shimmers in the sun during the day. At night, over 4,500 LED lights controlled by computer generate colors and images across the surface of the tower.

466 FT. (142 M) HIGH

MONSTERS ABOVE

GARGOYLES AROUND TOWN

Monsters and mythical creatures live high up in the Gothic and El Born districts – the oldest parts of town. Lots of scary-looking gargoyle drain spouts were put on medieval religious buildings over 600 years ago. The monsters and demons were meant to remind everybody of the eternal fight between good and evil. The mythical creatures, such as unicorns, come from ancient Catalan tales of brave knights battling magical foes.

4,500 WINDOWS

NEARLY 60,000 SHEETS OF GLASS

are tilted open or shut by computer to regulate the temperature inside the tower.

SCARY SKY CAR

Of the two cable car rides to try in Barcelona, Transbordador Aeri del Port is definitely the most exciting! It's very high, it doesn't stop, and there's nowhere to sit on the seven-minute journey between Barcelona's port and Montjuïc. The views are stunning, but it's not for those who are truly scared of heights!

MONTJUÏC
MUNICIPAL POOL

RIDE ESCALATORS, NOT BULLS

LAS ARENAS SHOPPING MALL

The city's second-oldest bullring was once filled with the roar of 16,000 fans, but bullfighting is now banned in Barcelona, and the ring has been made into a huge shopping mall. You can ride the escalators to the top for a fantastic view all across town, or for a dizzying look down at what was once the center of the bullring.

WORLD'S TOP SWIM

MONTJUÏC MUNICIPAL POOL

During the 1992 Olympics, this diving pool became world famous because of the stunning photos that showed divers in midair, with the city behind them. In July and August, anyone can swim in the pool, high up on Montjuïc. Because of its views, it's said to be one of the most spectacular swimming pools in the world.

THE CASTLE ON HIGH

MONTJUÏC CASTLE

MONTJUÏC CASTLE

One of the best views in town is up at Montjuïc Castle. It was built nearly 400 years ago and has played a part in several wars and rebellions since, its guns often pointing towards the town below to stop the townsfolk from rebelling. Now, the castle belongs to the city, and the giant guns on display face towards the sea, not inland. Though the castle has a violent history, it is now a much more peaceful place. It has its own movie and culture festival, and concerts are also held here.

MONTJUÏC GUNS

The castle was once armed with 120 cannons and had a moat around it. There are still some old Vickers guns, installed in 1938, on display at the castle. They fired shells out at enemy ships.

PRISON YEARS

During and after the Spanish Civil War, Montjuïc Castle had a dark history. It was a jail for prisoners on both sides of the rebellion led by General Franco. Many of them were executed by firing squad.

BEFORE THE CASTLE

Before the castle was built on Montjuïc, there was a lookout tower high up on the mountain that warned of approaching enemy ships. Long before that, the Ancient Romans quarried stone on Montjuïc to build their homes and temples. Even further back in time, prehistoric people lived on the castle site. They left some of their flint-making tools behind.

HERO WHO LOST HIS HEART

A CATALAN HERO, PRINCE GEORGE OF HESSEN-DARMSTADT DIED TRYING TO TAKE THE CASTLE FROM THE FRENCH IN 1705. HE IS BURIED IN BARCELONA BUT HIS HEART WAS SENT BACK TO DARMSTADT IN GERMANY, WHERE HE WAS BORN. HE HAS A BARCELONA STREET — CARRER DEL PRÍNCEP JORDI — NAMED AFTER HIM.

SURPRISE!

In 1705, during the War of the Spanish Succession, the British commander Lord Peterborough wanted to take Montjuïc Castle from the French and pro-French Spanish. His troops staged a diversion at the front of the castle while others secretly crept up to the back and successfully attacked.

568 FT. (173 M)
ABOVE SEA LEVEL

1640
THE YEAR THE FIRST CASTLE WAS BUILT

BARCELONA STYLE

Barcelona has a rich history of great design, not just in its buildings but in lots of different areas - from clothing to digital technology. Explore the design trail, and be inspired by one of Europe's most imaginative cities.

LA MANUAL ALPARGATERA

DIGITAL DARING

ARTS SANTA MÒNICA

This art and design center is at the cutting edge of art that uses digital technology. There is always something new and exciting to see and often things to participate in, too, from digital art and sound to music design and video games.

THE ARTS SANTA MÒNICA IS IN AN OLD CONVENT FOR NUNS KNOWN AS "BAREFOOT AUGUSTINES" (THEY WORE SANDALS INSTEAD OF SHOES TO SHOW THAT THEY LED A SIMPLE LIFE). WHAT WOULD THEY THINK OF DIGITAL ART AND ELECTRONIC MUSIC?!

CATALAN SHOE STYLE

LA MANUAL ALPARGATERA

Espadrilles are traditional Catalan shoes with rope soles. Many people wear them around town in summer and with traditional clothing at festival times. The oldest and most famous espadrille store in Barcelona is La Manual Alpargatera, which opened in 1940 and has been making the city's favorite foot fashion ever since.

START
ARTS SANTA MÒNICA

CATALAN COSTUMES

PLAÇA SANT JAUME AND OTHER FESTIVAL LOCATIONS

Traditional Catalan costumes are sometimes worn at festival times. For instance, you might see *bastoners*, traditional Catalan dancers who perform with sticks, wearing white with matching colored handkerchiefs around their necks and sashes round their waists.

THE TRADITIONAL CATALAN COSTUME FOR WOMEN IS A SKIRT AND WHITE TOP, AN APRON, AND A WHITE LACE HAT.

THE TRADITIONAL CATALAN COSTUME FOR MEN IS SHORT PANTS, A VEST, AND A FLOPPY RED HAT CALLED A *BARRETINA*.

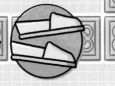

PLAÇA SANT JAUME

PASSEIG DE GRÀCIA

TOP TILES

PASSEIG DE GRÀCIA AND OTHER LOCATIONS

In Barcelona, design is everywhere, even under your feet. All across the city there are different types of street tiles called *panots* to see. Each district has its own tile style. The most well-known *panots* are the Flor de Barcelona, a four-petaled flower, and the Pedrera, which shows flowers and plants and was designed by Gaudí. The Passeig de Gràcia is the best place to spot Pedrera *panots*.

RED FLOR DE BARCELONA TILES MARK OUT THE MODERNISM ROUTE. THEY ARE FOUND IN FRONT OF KEY MODERNIST BUILDINGS.

SUITS YOU

MUSEU DEL DISSENY

Barcelona's Design Museum showcases the city's flair for design, from graphics and objects such as furniture to fashion through the ages. It has a fantastic collection of modern clothing and historical costumes, including two tunics that may date back as far as 1,700 years.

SUCCESSFUL FASHION COMPANIES MANGO AND MASSIMO DUTTI BOTH BEGAN IN BARCELONA.

BARCELONA IN YOUR HOME

BD BARCELONA DESIGN

The BD concept store is a huge warehouse shop that's almost the size of a museum. It sells lots of Barcelona-based design, includin reproductions of furniture created by famous artists. It's the place to buy chairs designed by Gaudí or a sofa like a giant pair of red lips designed by Salvador Dalí.

BD BARCELONA DESIGN

FASHION FRENZY

VENUES AROUND TOWN

During Barcelona's Fashion Week, designers showcase their outfits and compete for big awards. The world's fashion press lines the catwalk as models wear the hottest styles, soon to be in the stores.

search: ICONIC SPAIN

A FAN OF DESIGN

The Spanish fan is an iconic design with its own secret language...

- Holding a closed fan near your heart means "I love you."
- Hitting your hand with a closed fan means "Leave me alone."

SMART CITY

PARC DEL FÒRUM AND AROUND TOWN

Barcelona is celebrated for its innovative technology designs. Every year, it holds the Smart City Expo World, exploring new ideas for city living. It also uses lots of smart digital ideas to make life better for its city dwellers. For instance, it has the largest solar power installations in Europe, located in the Fòrum, which generates power for over 160,000 households.

BARCELONA'S HYBRID BUSES ARE SOME OF THE CLEANEST IN EUROPE. ITS BUS STOPS EVEN HAVE SOLAR-POWERED DISPLAYS.

IN SOME PARTS OF TOWN, PUBLIC TRASH CANS CAN NEVER OVERFLOW. THE GARBAGE DROPPED INTO THEM IS SUCKED UNDERGROUND AND SPEEDS THROUGH PIPES TO COLLECTION STATIONS.

CITY SURPRISES

Follow the pathway of amazement between some of the city's most unusual sights, from a deadly historical fountain to some chocolate model buildings and a clown who has been playing music for over a century.

START

JOAN MIRÓ FOUNDATION

CARRER NOU DE LA RAMBLA

WORLD'S DEADLIEST FOUNTAIN

MERCURY FOUNTAIN, JOAN MIRÓ FOUNDATION

In the 1930s, American sculptor Alexander Calder designed this fountain, which pumps pure mercury instead of water. Mercury is highly poisonous, but this wasn't known at the time. Now the fountain is on display behind glass so that visitors don't breathe in the fumes or touch the beautiful but deadly silvery stream.

MEMORIES OF A DIVIDED COUNTRY

AIR RAID SHELTER 307, CARRER NOU DE LA RAMBLA

During the Spanish Civil War, more than 190 bombing raids were made on Barcelona. Local people had to dig their own air raid shelters to hide from the rain of bombs. This one, now open to the public, was dug into the hillside of Montjuïc. It had room for around 2,000 people but they only had a couple of minutes to get there from their homes once the air raid sirens sounded. In the worst bombing raid, which took place in March 1938, over 1,000 people were killed in the city.

SUPERMAN'S SPOT

THE WAX MUSEUM

Superman lives down a small side street just off
La Rambla. Well, his waxwork does, along with
lots of other waxworks of famous characters and
celebrities. Here, you can come face-to-face with
some of the people we've mentioned in this book,
such as Picasso and Don Quixote. Superman,
meanwhile, is up on the roof, getting ready to
fly to someone's rescue!

200+
WAXWORKS
IN THE MUSEUM

CARRER DEL PARADÍS

WALKING WITH THE ROMANS

TEMPLE OF AUGUSTUS, CARRER DEL PARADÍS

Four huge columns stand in a hidden courtyard near the center of
town. They date back to over 2,000 years ago, when the Ancient
Romans founded Barcino, which was their name for Barcelona.
The columns were once part of the grand Temple of Augustus,
where Emperor Augustus was worshipped as a god. Roman priests
sacrificed animals to the gods here, then looked closely at the
animals' innards to help them predict the future.

CARRER PRINCESA

THAT'S MAG-EST-IC!

EL REI DE LA MÀGIA, CARRER PRINCESA

Step this way if you want to buy a magic wand. Barcelona has one of the oldest magic shops in the world, founded in 1881. It has its own magic school, magic museum, and workshop where new tricks are created. Its name means "the king of magic," and inside there are show posters and outfits used by some of the greatest magicians of the past. It's a great place for young magicians to pick up tips and secrets for their own successful magic show.

COLLECTION CRAZY

FREDERIC MARÈS MUSEUM, PLAÇA SANT IU

Frederic Marès was a collection-crazy sculptor who once lived in the city. His museum collections include scissors, toy soldiers, baby cribs, eyeglasses, keys, pipes, gloves, fans, brooches, playing cards, hat pins, train tickets, snuff boxes, watches, model cars, toy robots, rocking horses, puppet theater sets, walking sticks, dolls' houses, cameras, combs, jewelry, nutcrackers, perfume bottles, needle cases, embroidered wallets, and old bicycles!

MAGIC TRICKS WEREN'T ALWAYS WELCOME IN BARCELONA. IN MEDIEVAL TIMES, ANYBODY WHO PERFORMED A MAGIC TRICK RISKED BEING BURNED AT THE STAKE FOR SUPPOSEDLY BEING IN LEAGUE WITH THE DEVIL.

PLAÇA SANT IU

MMM...USEUM

MUSEU DE LA XOCOLATA, CARRER DEL COMERÇ

Cocoa was originally brought to Europe from Central America in the 1500s by Spanish invaders, and Barcelona was one of the first places where it arrived and was made into bars and hot drinks. This museum explains how chocolate is made and is famous for its incredible chocolate sculptures, including chocolate versions of famous buildings such as the Sagrada Família. The entrance ticket to the museum is a chocolate bar!

CARRER DEL COMERÇ

search: SWEET SECRET

📍 CHOCOLATE STASH

When the Spanish first brought back cocoa beans from Central America, they kept their chocolate treat a secret. English sailors who raided Spanish treasure ships threw the beans over the side because they thought they were sheep droppings.

TIBIDABO

MOVING MARVELS

MUSEU D'AUTOMATS, TIBIDABO

Before there were robots, we had automatons – mechanical models expertly made from lots of tiny, hidden moving parts. The museum has around 40 of these beautiful models, some new and some very old and rare. Its oldest model is a 130-year-old clown that can play a mandolin.

SPOTTED IN THE STREETS

There are lots of interesting things to spot out and about on the streets of Barcelona. This trail will help you discover the stories behind some of the city's stunning sights.

START

JOAN MIRÓ PARK

66 FT. (20 M) HIGH

LADY OF THE POND

WOMAN AND BIRD, JOAN MIRÓ PARK

One of Barcelona artist Miró's most famous sculptures sits reflected in a pool in a park named after him. It shows a female figure with a bird on her head. Originally, Miró was going to call it *Lady Mushroom with a Moon Hat*. He used birds in his work to symbolize the connection between Earth and the starry universe above. Find out more about Miró on page 56.

SYMBOLIC STONES

THE FOUR COLUMNS, PLAÇA D'ESPANYA

This mighty four-column sculpture has a hidden message to all Catalans. Its shape echoes the stripes on the Catalan flag, which makes it a symbol of Catalan freedom from Spanish rule. The columns were destroyed in 1928, but they were fully restored in 2011.

PLAÇA D'ESPANYA

FREDERIC MARÈS MUSEUM

EGGS-TRAORDINARY

DANCING EGGS, FREDERIC MARÈS MUSEUM AND AROUND TOWN

In early June, 60 days after Easter Sunday, you'll see something rather surprising dancing in the water jets of the fountains around old Barcelona. Eggs bob around in the jets for a festival called L'Ou Com Balla, which translates as "how the egg dances." The eggs have been dancing in the fountains for around 400 years, and nobody knows exactly why. One idea is that they might represent the renewal of life in springtime.

THE DANCING EGGS ARE FIRST PRICKED AND EMPTIED OF THEIR YOLK AND WHITE. THEN THEY ARE SEALED WITH WAX TO MAKE THEM JUST THE RIGHT WEIGHT TO STAY UP IN A WATER JET.

RAMBLA DEL RAVAL

FAT CAT

THE RAVAL CAT, RAMBLA DEL RAVAL

This big chubby cat was designed by Colombian sculptor Fernando Botero. People often try to climb on it, although it's harder to do than it looks. The cat has a friend by the same artist across town – a horse that stands welcoming people at Barcelona Airport.

23 FT. (7 M) LONG
6.6 FT. (2 M) HIGH

CARRER DE LES MOSQUES

58 IN.
(148 CM)
THE NARROWEST
► PART OF ◄
FLY STREET

A BUZZING CORNER OF TOWN

CARRER DE LES MOSQUES

Carrer de les Mosques is Barcelona's narrowest street. *Carrer* is the Catalan word for "street," and *mosques* is Catalan for "flies." The street got its name because long ago, it was always full of flies, attracted by the smells and food at a nearby market in El Born district. The market is now a cultural center, so thankfully the flies have moved on.

HOUSES OF HISTORY

EL BORN CENTRE DE CULTURA I MEMÒRIA

Old streets and houses from the 1700s can be seen here, as well as an exhibit of everyday objects, such as plates and jugs. The people who lived in the houses fled, leaving everything behind, when Barcelona was besieged and fell to Spanish forces in 1714.

EL BORN CENTRE DE CULTURA I MEMÒRIA

CATALONIA WAS INVADED BY SPANISH KING PHILIP V AND DEFEATED ON SEPTEMBER 11, 1714. CATALONIA LOST ITS INDEPENDENCE TO SPAIN ON THAT DAY. THE DATE IS MARKED EVERY YEAR AS THE NATIONAL DAY OF CATALONIA.

HIDDEN FIGURE

THE BARCELONA HEAD, PORT VELL

Outdoor art is popular around Barcelona, and down by the sea, US pop artist Roy Lichtenstein has added his contribution. It's a giant comic-book head covered with broken tiles, Gaudi-style.

LOOK CLOSELY AT THE BARCELONA HEAD TO FIND A SECOND CRAZY-LOOKING FIGURE. THE BLUE EYE AND NOSE OF THE BIG FACE IS ALSO THE ARM AND BODY OF A STRANGE SKULL-LIKE CHARACTER PEEKING OUT WITH YELLOW EYES.

ROOM WITH A VIEW

BARCELONETA ART

There's a famous statue on Barceloneta beach. It shows a pile of rusty metal cubes on top of each other, like the wobbly floors of an old building. It's a tribute to the old fishing district that has been cleared away and replaced by modern Barceloneta.

DOWN BY THE BEACH AT BARCELONETA, THERE ARE FIVE ODD-LOOKING PEOPLE IN LONG RAINCOATS STANDING IN A CAGE IGNORING EACH OTHER. THE FIGURES ARE MADE OF BRONZE, HAVE SPHERICAL BASES AND ARE PART OF A MYSTERIOUS SCULPTURE CALLED A *ROOM WHERE IT ALWAYS RAINS*. IT WAS CREATED BY JUAN MUÑOZ, AND THE CAGE IS SAID TO HAVE BEEN INSPIRED BY THE UMBRACLE — A GREENHOUSE IN CIUTADELLA PARK.

77

POINTING TO THE PAST

COLUMBUS MONUMENT

At the foot of La Rambla, there's a giant man pointing out to sea. He is the 15th-century explorer, Christopher Columbus, who sailed west to find a new route to Asia. Instead, he accidentally found the islands of the Caribbean and the Americas. At first, he famously thought he'd reached India.

NOBODY REALLY KNOWS WHAT COLUMBUS LOOKED LIKE BECAUSE NO PORTRAITS WERE MADE OF HIM DURING HIS LIFETIME.

WHICH WAY?

Some people mistakenly assume that Christopher Columbus is pointing towards America. In fact, he's pointing towards North Africa. The sculptor wanted him to point in the general direction of the sea.

ROYAL BACKERS

THE SPANISH KING FERDINAND AND QUEEN ISABELLA FUNDED COLUMBUS ON HIS FIRST VOYAGE. WHEN HE RETURNED, HE DOCKED IN BARCELONA TO MEET THEM. HE IS THOUGHT TO HAVE GONE IN A PROCESSION TO THE PLAÇA DEL REI, WHERE HE PRESENTED THE MONARCHS WITH THINGS HE'D BROUGHT BACK FROM HIS TRIP, INCLUDING GOLD, PINEAPPLES, TOBACCO PLANTS, AND A HAMMOCK. HE ALSO BROUGHT BACK A GROUP OF PEOPLE HE HAD CAPTURED AS SLAVES IN THE CARIBBEAN

COLUMBUS MONUMENT

YOU CAN TAKE AN ELEVATOR TO A VIEWING PLATFORM JUST UNDER COLUMBUS'S GIANT FEET FOR A VIEW AROUND TOWN.

197 FT. (60 M) HIGH

18 IN. (45.7 CM)

THE LENGTH OF THE STATUE'S **FINGER**

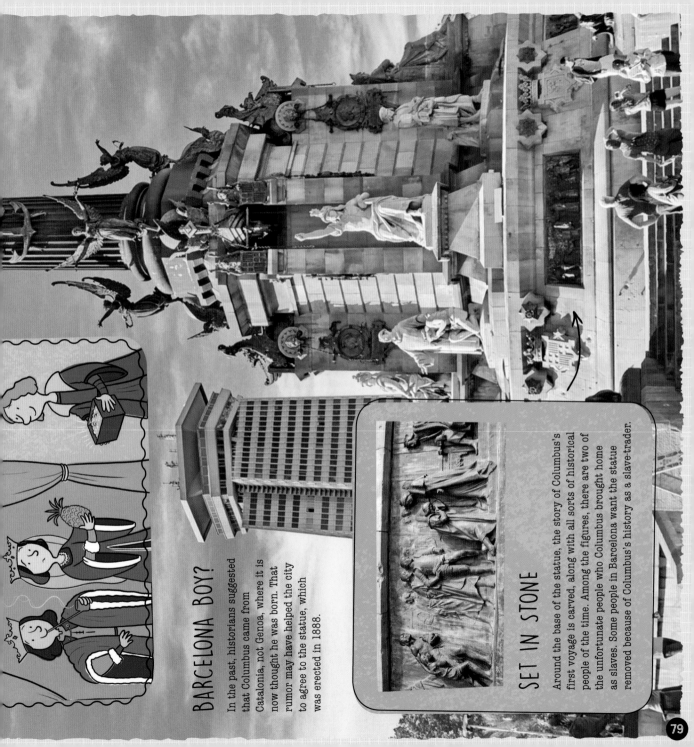

BARCELONA BOY?

In the past, historians suggested that Columbus came from Catalonia, not Genoa, where it is now thought he was born. That rumor may have helped the city to agree to the statue, which was erected in 1888.

SET IN STONE

Around the base of the statue, the story of Columbus's first voyage is carved, along with all sorts of historical people of the time. Among the figures, there are two of the unfortunate people who Columbus brought home as slaves. Some people in Barcelona want the statue removed because of Columbus's history as a slave-trader.

SPOOKY STUFF

The old parts of Barcelona have lots of ghostly legends and stories of scary goings-on in days gone by. Take the spooky ghost walk to find out more.

GOING OUT IN STYLE

MUSEU DE CARROSSES FÚNEBRES

The museum of funeral carriages shows visitors how the dead were buried in Barcelona, especially in the 1800s. You can see some of the fancy horsedrawn hearses used to carry the coffins to their final resting place. They look like scary versions of fairytale coaches.

MUSEU DE CARROSSES FÚNEBRES

DEFEATING THE DEVIL

SANTA MARIA DEL PI BASILICA

This pretty church was once visited by the devil, according to legend. It's said that when the builder ran out of stone to finish the tower, the devil appeared and offered him the stone in return for his soul. He'd have to surrender his soul once he'd built the hundredth step in the tower and thus finished the church. The builder took the stone but only built 99 steps and saved himself from the devil.

SANTA MARIA DEL PI BASILICA

EMOTIONAL POTION

THE ALCHEMIST'S HOUSE, CARRER DE L'ARC DE SANT RAMON DEL CALL

Legend has it that a medieval alchemist (a maker of potions) once lived at number eight on this street. His daughter fell in love with a nobleman and met him secretly, completely unknown to her father. When she changed her mind and rejected the nobleman, he tricked the unknowing father into making him a bouquet laced with deadly poisons, which he gave to the girl. When she smelled it and died, her heartbroken father fled the city, cursing his house.

FOR CENTURIES, THE ALCHEMIST'S HOUSE WAS LEFT EMPTY BECAUSE OF THE TERRIBLE TALE OF THE CURSE. NOWADAYS, IT'S AN INFORMATION CENTER ON THE JEWISH COMMUNITY OF BARCELONA.

MURDERER ADULTERER WITCH

SCARY SHOES

THE EXECUTIONER'S HOUSE, PLAÇA DEL REI

By tradition, Barcelona's executioner lived in a small house here. He also got some other more gruesome perks with the job. He could sell the bodies of prisoners for medical use, and he could sell their clothes and shoes, too. The footwear brought in good money because locals believed that an executed person's shoes would ward away evil spirits if put at the entrance to a house.

WITCH SCHOOL
CARRER DE LA NEU
DE SANT CUGAT

The medieval authorities of Barcelona used to accuse people of witchcraft and burn them at the stake! Professional witch hunters rounded up suspects — many were women who used herbs for medicine. Rumor has it that there was once an ancient witchcraft school on this spot and that some of its students were caught and burned by the authorities.

ROPEY JOB
CARRER DELS CORDERS

The name of this street translates as "rope-makers' street." The town's rope-makers were shunned by people because they made the hangman's noose for executions. They weren't allowed in churches, and it was said that they had devilish powers such as unnatural ear wiggling. If they spat on the floor, it was said that worms grew out of their spit.

SOMETIMES THE RELATIVES OF CONDEMNED PRISONERS WOULD BRIBE THE TOWN'S ROPE-MAKERS INTO MAKING A WEAK ROPE. IF IT BROKE DURING A HANGING, THE PRISONER WOULD BE PARDONED.

CREEPY CREATURES

OLD BARCELONA NATURAL SCIENCES MUSEUM, CIUDTADELLA PARK

The old Natural Sciences Museum is said to be haunted by the animals that were once displayed here! In the past, museum guards were apparently scared off by the weird night noises of the supposed spooky creatures. Awooooooooo!

THE OLD MUSEUM BULIDING IS KNOWN AS CASTELL DELS TRES DRAGONS (CASTLE OF THE THREE DRAGONS), AND IT WAS BUILT FOR THE PARK'S BIG EXHIBIT IN 1888. DRAGONS NEVER LIVED THERE REALLY... OR SO THEY SAY. PERHAPS THEY'RE ASLEEP SOMEWHERE NEARBY!

PLAÇA DE SANT PERE

KNIGHT NIGHT

PLAÇA DE SANT PERE

It's not surprising that there are lots of ghost stories linked to the oldest parts of town, and in this corner, there is said to be a wandering ghost called Pere Pals. The story goes that he was a medieval knight who fell in love with a nun in the convent here. He tried to visit her but got killed by ghostly wolves as punishment for daring to love her. He's said to wander around, still looking for his lost lady.

search: SPOOKY PLACES

PLAÇA DEL COMERÇ This small square has a large clock and a streetlamp in the middle of it. Some say you can see ghosts crossing in the light of the streetlamp at night.

CARRER DE LA FLOR DE LLIRI This street once had lots of inns for travelers. Legend says many guests disappeared in mysterious circumstances and were never found again.

INDEX

INDEX

FURTHER READING

The Cities Book
Lonely Planet Kids

Packed with facts about Barcelona and other cities around the world, this book tells you what it's like to grow up in a different country. It covers festivals, history, architecture, and more to give you the insider's view of Barcelona.

Miró's Magic Animals
by Antony Penrose

When the author was a boy, Miró came to visit his parents in England. This magical book about art makes connections between photographs of this visit and Miró's work.

Mission Barcelona:
A Scavenger Hunt Adventure
by Catherine Aragon

This book sends the whole family on a fact-finding journey around Barcelona. With a total of 13 missions, it can be used as a guide to Barcelona and is great for discovering hidden treasures.

First Words: Spanish
Lonely Planet Kids

Aimed at younger children, this book is a fantastic introduction to the Spanish language. Full of handy words to use while on vacation, each word has an easy-to-understand pronunciation guide.

Antoni Gaudí Colouring Book
Prestel

With short bursts of text and lots of images of Gaudí's masterpieces, this book can be used to identify and engage with Barcelona's buildings, whether you're visiting the city or experiencing it from home.

50 Fun Things To Do in Barcelona
by Sarah Berry

Crammed with activities for kids, this book visits six of the most popular places in Barcelona. The activities follow the layout of the places and encourage kids to explore the city in depth.